THE LEWES FLOOD

by Andy Thomas, with a foreword by Norman Baker MP

Photos by Andy Thomas & Beth Tandy, with Stephen Crowhurst, Michael Priest, Liz Kaye ARPS, Sussex Express & Jenny Keen

ACKNOWLEDGMENTS

First published in 2001 by S B Publications
19 Grove Road, Seaford, East Sussex, BN25 1TP
Tel: 01323 893498/Fax: 01323 893860
e-mail: sales@sbpublications.swinternet.co.uk

Reprinted October 2001

Photographs by Andy Thomas and Beth Tandy,
with Stephen Crowhurst, Michael Priest, Liz Kaye ARPS,
Sussex Express and Jenny Keen.
All images Copyright of the photographers.

ISBN 1-85770-236-0

Typeset and printed by:

Tansleys The Printers
19 Broad Street, Seaford,
East Sussex, BN25 1LS
Tel: 01323 891019
e-mail: TansleysTP@aol.com

*Andy Thomas would like to express huge thanks
to the following:*

All the photographers, of course, for their help and
co-operation; everyone at Tansleys and S B Publications,
Rupert Taylor, Hugh Rowlings, John Eccles, Mark Hazelby,
Denise Miller and camera crew at the *Sussex Express;* all the
retailers who agreed to reduce their percentage to aid the
book's charitable purpose; John Magness and David
Waddington of the Lewes Flood Appeal for their help and
contribution; Hope Pym of *Private Eye* for helpful permission
to use their quote; Kaye Thomas for proof-reading; and
especially Norman Baker MP for his kind foreword.

Other books by Andy Thomas:

Fields of Mystery
Quest For Contact (with Paul Bura)
Vital Signs
Streets of Fire
Prehistoric Sacred Sites of Wessex Vol. II:
Devon and Cornwall (with Kent Goodman)

"And when the Sun comes out,
After this rain shall stop,
A wondrous light will fill
Each dark, round drop;
I hope the Sun shines bright;
'Twill be a lovely sight."

W H DAVIES, *The Rain*

CONTENTS

FOREWORD

by Norman Baker MP

The floods which hit Lewes last October came and went quickly, but they will last in the local memory for many years to come. It was awesome to witness the power of nature sweeping incredible quantities of water into the town. It was heartbreaking to see the resultant devastation which became painfully obvious when the waters receded.

In the hours before the flood, there was an uneasy air about the town. Quite a few gathered on Cliffe Bridge, watching the water rise. It looked touch and go. And then so much more water arrived so quickly. It overcame walls, rushed through gaps, and in minutes rather than hours, the centre of the town was under water. I remember seeing the cars in the Safeway car park, which had been moved round to the bus station side for protection, and which soon were trapped, up to their roofs in water. All of Cliffe was under water bar the tiniest section of road at the top of the bridge. Eventually the water even lapped up School Hill.

The next day, as I made my way around town to see what I could do to help, it became obvious the damage was enormous, particularly in the Malling area. I recall visiting houses in Spences Lane where the water had even reached first floor level. Suddenly, 400 households were homeless, and much of the retail and industrial areas of the town had been wrecked.

Yet through all this, people remained amazingly cheerful and positive, as they set about rebuilding their lives. The authorities, especially Lewes District Council, responded really well to the disaster, and I think that helped the morale of the town. Since then, many individuals from near and far have contributed generously to the Lewes Flood Appeal, where profits from this book will also go.

Almost a year on, interest from the national media has long gone, but the consequences of the flood are still with us. Many people have still not been able to return to their homes. Some shops and businesses remain shut. We must continue as a town to help them. But it has been great to see how Lewes has picked itself up and bounced back. It is proof of the deep community spirit and underlying strength of the town.

Now the challenge is to ensure the town gets the proper flood defences it needs and that the 2000 flood is never allowed to happen again.

NORMAN BAKER
May 2001

Norman Baker is Liberal Democrat MP for Lewes.

INTRODUCTION

The night of 12th October 2000 was a disturbing one. Pulling the bedcovers over my head couldn't shut out the noise of rain battering the roof and window so hard it felt as if it were going to break into the room. Worryingly, it continued all night.

Next morning, the flowerbed had vanished under a pool of brown water and a new stream snaked across the garden and down the side of the house, narrowly missing the front door. Nevertheless, the school run beckoned and my six-year old son and I got dressed and ate breakfast as we would any other morning. Outside, we discovered the car was somewhat inaccessible due to a barrier of large wooden planks which had been placed across our sloping village car park. Neighbours were trying to stop a torrent of water flowing down from the main road into their houses. Allowing me to move the car, they needn't have bothered as we didn't get more than a mile or so before traffic ground to a halt due to the road suddenly disappearing beneath a river where there hadn't been one before. It slowly dawned that this was going to be one extraordinary day. A U-turn enabled us to double back for the relative safety of home.

As the morning wore on and we absorbed the television and radio reports telling of watery disaster, I began to find myself wondering how the Ouse Valley was coping and decided to drive the short journey into Lewes to find out. From the Offham Road, the transformed scenery of inundated fields unfolded. It was quite clear that my home town was in trouble.

But disaster hadn't struck just yet. I made it into town, where there was a bustling air of anticipation. The lunch-time skies had cleared a little and Cliffe Bridge had become a viewing balcony, as people clustered upon it to see the Ouse at a level not witnessed in Lewes for many years, perhaps since the 1960 floods. Thankful that the river had stopped just short of swamping the street, I strolled nonchalantly through the shops.

As I browsed in Dixons, a staff member calmly strode to the door and called for everyone in the shop to leave. High tide was approaching and a 25 minute flood warning had been given... Shoppers were politely driven from Cliffe precinct. At this point I realised history was in the making, so I drove home again, picked up my camera and headed back into town...

Perhaps it sounds ghoulish now, but I was far from the only one with the same idea, and I feel it right that I was present to witness a quite remarkable, if harrowing, moment in the annals of Lewesian life, which it is the place of this book to record.

This document of what happened to Lewes on October 12th 2000 and the days following is achieved largely through photographs taken by myself and an unconnected group of people who found themselves with cameras in the right places at the right times. There must be many people across Lewes with excellent photographic records of their own, but it would be an impossible task to compile them all, so unavoidably this is a selective, yet comprehensive, telling of the events of the Lewes flood, with some complementary text. I have not forgotten, incidentally, that other Sussex towns were also badly hit, but those stories are for others to tell.

Like me, the book's other principal photographer Beth Tandy prowled the streets during and after the main events, as, of course, did the intrepid *Sussex Express* crew. Others, like Stephen Crowhurst and Michael Priest, both Harveys Brewery staff, found themselves at the centre of the drama and were lucky to have a digital camera to hand to capture the events:

"We were trapped upstairs with about five feet of water downstairs. We were taking pictures of everything we could see. We did not realise the full extent of what was happening because all we could see was a very small part of Lewes - we were almost like an island. By the end of the day we were glad to see the rescue boat coming into the yard to take us home. This was a day we will never forget and hope will never be repeated."

Liz Kaye, a Cliffe High Street resident, also found herself 'on the spot':

"Having refused offers of rescue from the fire crews and lifeboat men, I sat out a very eerie 24 hours watching the waters rise and fall, sensing a very strange isolation. Even stranger was the following morning when the waters had dropped back to welly-boot level - the police had cordoned off the area to stop looters and I wandered about what felt like a ghost town with my camera, recording images for my friends and neighbours."

The book is not a technical manual of how the flood took place, nor gives exact timings of the events. Rather, it is an impression of what life was like for Lewesians during the crisis and displays how familiar landmarks and scenery looked in such unusual and spectacular circumstances. With this in mind, photos taken on different days of the flood's active duration (largely October 12th and 13th) and the aftermath are sometimes mixed together as appropriate, yet the book does follow a loose chronology of sorts and employs a logically structured travelogue through the town for those who care to look for it. Inevitably, there are one or two affected areas of Lewes the book doesn't cover, but the main bones of the event are present.

To mitigate accusations of voyeuristically cashing in on a disaster that brought so much psychological and financial misery to so many (fully recognised in the text), profits from this book are being donated to the Lewes Flood Appeal, the function of which is described on page 50. All the photographers have donated their work free of charge and the printers have generously reduced their fees. We and everyone at S B Publications hope this tome will raise enough money to help assist those still in need of compensation and stir attention to the urgent requirement of sturdier flood prevention measures in an age of climatic uncertainty.

Let us hope there need never be a sequel to this book!

ANDY THOMAS

The new-look Ouse Valley as seen from Kingsley Road, Landport (Andy Thomas)

Clockwise from lower left: i) Concerned Lewesians at Kingsley Road (Andy Thomas)   ii) View from the air as the Ouse oozes... (Sussex Express)   iii) Crowds gather at Kingsley Road (Andy Thomas)

OUSE VALLEY: Lunch-time, Thursday October 12th. The word is out - Lewes is in trouble. For any travellers heading south towards the town along the A275 Offham Road or the B2192 from Ringmer, the Ouse Valley is a dramatic pointer to what must lie further on. The familiar curves and lines of the river itself have vanished, as the sludge-tinged waters have flowed over the banks and levelled out across the grazing land into a single great expanse, drowning farmland, plants - and cattle.

Lewes has become an estuary. The flood laps the edge of the Landport estate and begins to seep into houses on the lower slopes... Crowds start to gather at the top of Kingsley Road to gaze down across Landport in awe at the sight before them. What will escape today? If the Ouse Valley has suffered so, what has or will become of the town centre? Yet even now the floods still seem just a scenic novelty...

The Ouse swells ominously as dark clouds loom (Beth Tandy)

Anticlockwise from upper right: i & ii) The riverside path to Tesco disappears under the Ouse, swollen by rain and high tide (Jenny Keen) iii & iv) Floating debris ranges from innocuous to dangerous (Beth Tandy)   v) Shopping trolleys block the unwary from the riverside path (Andy Thomas)

FLOTSAM & JETSAM: And so to the town centre... Here the stately sweep of the Ouse beside Tesco has become an overwhelming swell, swallowing the footpath, yet never, curiously, Tesco itself. Equipment basements aside, it miraculously escapes by inches, though food is lost when cut power thaws refrigeration units.

The swell surges under the Phoenix Causeway and onto Cliffe Bridge. As the bloated tide passes, objects are swept along by the current, tree branches, unexpected and poignant domestic objects, chairs, refuse and chemical containers from the now inundated Phoenix industrial estate. There are animals, too, fighting to keep their heads above the surface - small rodents, rats, mice, voles... A small group of caring people hold out branches to them as they pass and manage to rescue a number. But the water carries other less harmless, invisible things, too. Chemicals and effluent...

Water touches Cliffe Bridge and surges into the streets (Andy Thomas)

Anticlockwise from upper right: i) Causeway spectators as seen from flooded Harveys (Stephen Crowhurst/Michael Priest) ii) On the Phoenix Causeway (Andy Thomas) iii) Grim faces as the enormity of the disaster begins to sink in (Beth Tandy) iv) The Causeway closed, the next day (Andy Thomas)

VIEW FROM THE CAUSEWAY: People are gathering in large numbers along the length of the Phoenix Causeway to watch the strange spectacle of Harveys Brewery being drowned and Cliffe Bridge touched by water. There is almost a party atmosphere at this point - large grins on people's faces are not uncommon, as they savour the novel anarchy of the moment. For a while it feels like an aquatic Bonfire Night as an odd kind of freedom-of-the-streets spirit prevails, before the police get to grips with clearing people away from what *they* recognise as a disaster area.

After a while, though, the gravity of the event begins to take hold and the grins subside when people begin to realise that homes are being destroyed and businesses wrecked. The Causeway is soon closed off. Even by late night, a surprising amount of sightseers are still drawn to the town centre, but turned away by road blocks and police guards.

Contaminated beer and tumbling barrels as the Ouse invades Harveys Brewery (Andy Thomas)

Staff retreat to the rooftops and balconies of Harveys Brewery as the water rises, leaving chaos in its wake. (Lower pictures: Stephen Crowhurst/Michael Priest. Upper pictures: Beth Tandy)

CHAOS AT HARVEYS: From the Phoenix Causeway, it's plain to see the scale of the disaster befalling Harveys Brewery. Onlookers gape as water finally tips over the wall. Metal barrels and fork-lift crates tumble, while machinery slowly submerges.

Inside, the invading surge sends brewery workers scurrying up stairs and onto rooftops for refuge as their workshops and storage areas fill up with a liquid not unlike certain ales in colour, but of a rather less palatable nature. Equipment is ruined, as other affected businesses also discover. A brew, however, fermenting this day and subsequently left longer than intended, survives intact and becomes a powerful mix. It is later sold to raise money for the Flood Appeal. 'Ouse Booze' sells fast!

The Riverside Lodge surgery finds its name becoming a little too literal... (Andy Thomas)

Clockwise from middle: i & ii) Rescue teams arrive as cars go under in the Malling Street car park (Beth Tandy) iii) The Riverside Lodge tries in vain to block the torrents (Beth Tandy) iv) The Phoenix Centre becomes an island, as seen from Harveys roof (Stephen Crowhurst/Michael Priest) v) Malling Street folk watch helplessly, stranded on upper floors (Beth Tandy)

SUNKEN PHOENIX: The Phoenix car park has become a lake, several feet high. In scenes repeated across eastern Lewes, cars react erratically to submersion; windscreen wipers operate by themselves and automatic windows wind absurdly up and down as water invades the electrics. Many cars, engines ruined, are written off by the flood.

The Riverside Lodge surgery and the Phoenix Centre are major casualties of the inundation, and the Jireh Chapel, only relatively recently restored, is also affected. Malling Street residents find themselves in need of rescue.

Thumbs up from the rescue crew at Malling Street (Beth Tandy)

Clockwise from middle: i) The rescue helicopter thunders over the town (Andy Thomas)   ii) The RNLI go swimming in Malling Street (Beth Tandy)   iii) The surreal experience of cruising down Cliffe High Street and into South Street (Liz Kaye)   iv) The determined face of an RNLI crew member (Beth Tandy)   v) Taxi, anyone..? (Liz Kaye)

RESCUE: For much of the afternoon, the hills and buildings around Lewes reverberate with the thundering of the large rescue helicopter overhead, co-ordinating courses for the intrepid RNLI boatmen in the Venice-like streets and, in some cases (page 43), actually hauling people up from the torrents.

The boat rescue crews themselves have their work cut out, helping trapped people from houses and cruising the town on reconnaissance missions. Today, only they have freedom of movement in a community which suddenly feels very different to its usual self. Their faces are at once determined and yet content, carrying out the job they are trained for. They are a reassuring presence for many traumatized residents.

Sodden kneeling-pads at St Thomas's Church, Cliffe... the result of 'God's punishment'? (Beth Tandy)

Upper pictures: Unholy water..? St Thomas's Church is deluged as residents and clergy escape into Cliffe High Street (Liz Kaye) Lower picture: The messy internal aftermath (Beth Tandy)

'GOD'S PUNISHMENT': To the floods, nothing is sacred. The water soaks believers and heathens alike, and there's little holy about it. St Thomas's Church at the South Street end of Cliffe suffers especially badly.

An ex-Lewes resident and well-known prophet of imminent 'end times', Matthew Dumbrell, enrages many in the days after with his over-publicised claim that the floods were God's punishment on the people of Lewes *"for not recognising his favoured son"* and for ignoring Dumbrell's earlier - and unfulfilled - predictions of doom. Why the Divine Creator should single out Lewesians in particular to inflict his vengeance on is never made quite clear...

Morris Road as the waters begin to recede (Liz Kaye)

The sad scene at Morris Road, repeated in too many other streets, as people clear up, trying to come to terms with what has happened, whilst salvaging the few things they can (Beth Tandy)

STREET SPIRIT?: The personal and psychological devastation wreaked on people is perhaps the most damaging aspect to the flood. Chemical and sewage effluence in the water leaves everything it touches contaminated beyond use, even when dried out.

Morris Road, off Cliffe High Street, is one of the areas badly hit. Here, as in other affected places, ruined furniture, domestic appliances and personal belongings are stacked up outside, ready to be taken away by refuse collectors for final disposal.

An unhappy shopper regrets overstaying in Safeway car park... (Beth Tandy)

Clockwise from lower left: i) Car moorings at Safeway... (Andy Thomas) ii) Piggy-back rides are at a premium (Beth Tandy) iii) Even trolleys have to go in the destructive wake of the polluted waters (Beth Tandy) iv) The chaos left at the main entrance (Andy Thomas)

NOT-SO-SAFEWAY: While rival Tesco escapes by the skin of its teeth across the other side of the Ouse, Safeway isn't so lucky. Water enters like a tidal wave and comes up through drains with surprising force, scattering tin cans, boxes and even heavy containers. Long-stay shoppers and staff find their cars quickly submerged in the same autogeddon which destroys engines, electrics and upholstery across the lower parts of Lewes.

In the weeks which follow, even after the damp food has gone, everything from the shop, trolleys, baskets *et al,* is disposed of in skips and bins. Car park prefabs provide a small retail outlet before a new updated and improved Safeway rises again from its messy, unexpected flushing out.

Ambulances patrol as police prevent sightseers entering the rapidly filling Cliffe precinct (Andy Thomas)

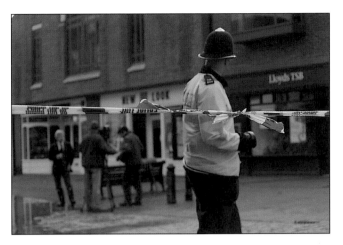

Clockwise from middle: i) Much as police try to discourage it, some still stroll nonchalantly around (Beth Tandy)   ii) As the waters recede from the Cliffe precinct, new boundaries are defined (Andy Thomas)   iii) The constabulary in South Street aren't in the mood to get their own feet wet, though (Liz Kaye) iv) A patrol car makes an impenetrable road block at Eastgate Street (Andy Thomas)   v) Makeshift repairs suggest the plastic barriers are rather less robust... (Andy Thomas)

THE ARM OF THE LAW: As eastern Lewes fills with water, so it also fills with sightseers, eager to catch a glimpse of this novel disaster affecting the town. But the police are on hand to block roads with patrol vehicles and mark boundaries with thin plastic tapes. The tapes regularly tear as crowds press ever-closer to see events for themselves, and the thin barriers are soon knotted with makeshift repairs.

Like the other emergency services, the police are also on hand to help stranded residents and keep some kind of order in the waterlogged streets. Firemen and ambulance crews are vital contributors to the rescue efforts, of course, in addition to the ubiquitous RNLI.

The things the media do to get an 'angle'... A TV reporter wades into now shallower waters at Cliffe precinct (Andy Thomas)

Clockwise from lower right: i & ii) Television broadcast vans in Friars Walk beam images of the Lewes inundation out to waiting satellites and back into our sets (Andy Thomas) iii) Another TV reporter makes the best of a suitably wet and bustling backdrop at the entrance to Malling Street (Jenny Keen) iv) The television vans jostle for position with fire engines... (Andy Thomas)

THE EYES OF THE WORLD: Suddenly, for a short and inglorious moment, Lewes has become the centre of media attention. Other places, such as Uckfield, share some unfortunate limelight, but Lewes is recognised as being one of the worst flood-hit areas in the country (800 properties affected, later statistics show). The images are beamed out into space from dish-laden vans and back again for broadcast around the world.

Faces which usually sit cozily on the glowing boxes in our living rooms are suddenly flesh and blood beings wandering about our local town, as well-known television reporters don wellingtons to wade for the viewers' delight. Radio and press also attend, and familiar voices from down the road are unexpectedly present in the airwaves, recounting their tales.

Bookshelf devastation at W H Smith (Beth Tandy)

Clockwise from middle: i - iv) Greetings cards, books, magazines and comics lie battered and forlorn inside W H Smith (Beth Tandy)   v) The waters surround the shop, but have already receded substantially in this photo - the original height is indicated by the darker line just visible on the redbrick wall (Andy Thomas)

BLACK BOOKS: As the waters flood into Cliffe High Street and the precinct, helpless shop staff have to evacuate or simply watch as rapidly rising currents flow unstoppably across carpets, sweeping items from shelves and soaking everything in their path.

The scene at W H Smith is typical of the devastation left in many shops. Three feet or so of muddy, contaminated liquid is no good for anything, especially magazines and books. Even items on higher shelves are ruined as the dampness curls and warps. Everything has to be destroyed and rooms redecorated - ironically so at W H Smith, and Forfars too, which have both only recently undergone complete re-fits. Second re-fits follow... Other shops remain closed for months. Some businesses threaten not to return in the event of another flood.

Stevenson's mirrored across the Friars Walk car park (Andy Thomas)

Flooded passageway at Harveys Brewery (Stephen Crowhurst/Michael Priest)

Clockwise from middle: i) Unexpected rapids near the Riverside Lodge surgery (Beth Tandy) ii) The side of Safeway at Eastgate Wharf (Andy Thomas) iii) A closer view - somewhere under here is a car park (Beth Tandy) iv) The same area as seen from Phoenix Causeway (Andy Thomas)

WATERWORLD: Those familiar little places never really thought about but forever frequented, car parks, passageways, side-streets, have become alien waterscapes. The town takes on a new feeling, as if one has entered a slightly altered dimension, not very different from our own but paved with liquid.

Denied access to certain areas by the increasing amounts of blue and white police tape, some feel unpleasantly cut off from parts of the town they know and love and wonder how unseen restricted quarters are coping - and what they look like in their new state.

The Pells playpark takes a bath... (Jenny Keen)

Clockwise from middle: i) A lone photographer surveys the scene at the Pells playpark (Jenny Keen) ii) The waters have risen to conceal the walkways completely (Jenny Keen) iii) Brook Street takes on a literal meaning... (Andy Thomas) iv) The playpark gates stand resolutely shut (Andy Thomas) v) Avenues of water-rooted trees at Pelham Terrace create an almost impressionistic scene, but the scummy swirls on the surface reveal the presence of unwelcome pollution (Beth Tandy)

PELLS POOLS: From the air (page 9) the sedate waterways of the Pells have simply become part of the nearby Ouse. On the ground, the pavements have vanished, the famous outdoor swimming pool has been absorbed and the playpark is visible only by its walls and gateway.

Even the ducks and moorhens, which traditionally parade themselves on the banks or swim nonchalantly by, seem to have retreated to drier habitats. The waters which host their usual frolics are now tainted with chemicals and sewage. But the Pells area remains unrestricted and visitors flock to see a different sight today.

The main railway line to London, behind Talbot Terrace... (Andy Thomas)

Talbot Terrace itself fared little better... (Andy Thomas)

Clockwise from lower left: i) The Phoenix industrial estate goes under (Jenny Keen)   ii) Families gaze at the new-look Talbot Terrace (Andy Thomas)   iii) One way of drying out a pair of boots... on school railings at Talbot Terrace (Beth Tandy)   iv) A road divided... Toronto Terrace residents find themselves stranded on the wrong side (Andy Thomas)

A RIVER RUNS THROUGH IT...: From the Pells, the flow continues into Talbot Terrace and across Toronto Terrace, which finds itself cut in two by the new river, stranding residents on the cul-de-sac side. The water also leaks directly into the main Lewes to London railway cutting, covering the tracks completely.

Talbot Terrace homeowners find fate dealing uneven blows - some houses have their lower floors inundated, while others, some only next door but raised just a few inches higher, escape almost unscathed. Similar scenes are repeated elsewhere. Filled cellars take weeks to pump out.

No petrol today... Emergency services get waterlogged at Malling Street (Sussex Express)

Scenes of havoc, during and after inundation, from Spences Lane and Malling... Even ambulance crews don't escape the flooding (Sussex Express)

MALLING: The lower areas of this part of Lewes are defenceless, as the Ouse tips over the old flood plains, perilously built on in more recent years. Today, tempted fate calls its debts in.

Spences Lane is particularly badly hit, and in extreme cases some houses find water almost up to the top floors. This is where much of the television reportage centres itself and the RNLI have their heaviest work followed by cameras. Certainly, the scenes are shocking, but other streets with less attention are also deluged.

An ambulance crew find themselves cut off during a rescue mission and have no choice but to abandon their vehicle to the flood. Other emergency vehicles are caught out in similar scenes elsewhere, water rising alarmingly in the few minutes their drivers leave them to carry out their duties with distressed residents.

The Lewes to London canal line... (Andy Thomas)

Clockwise from lower left: i) The Harveys yard at Pinwell Road becomes a lake, as seen from Station Road ii) Looking west across the platforms to the aptly named Tanner's Brook iii & iv) A shock awaits long-distance commuters on their eventual return to the station car park... (Andy Thomas)

PLATFORM BLUES: The main Eastbourne to London railway line becomes an ideal drainage conduit for the flood as the rails slowly submerge, leaving a sight which bears a remarkable resemblance to a canalway. Lewes station even finds itself on the cover of the satirical magazine *Private Eye* the following week, with a caption bubble reading *"The boat arriving on Platform 3 is the delayed 3.36 from Hastings"*, together with other droll remarks. With track repairs and the shoring up of ballast subsidence, it takes weeks for services to return to normality.

The station car park plays host to yet further mechanical casualties of events, and some overnight commuters find themselves unable to return to Lewes, left wondering about the fate of their prized vehicles. Meanwhile, residents at the nearby and relatively new Tanner's Brook unexpectedly discover a depressing old meaning to their street name...

The astonishing watery landscape looking out to Hamsey, as seen from Offham Road (Andy Thomas)

Clockwise from lower left: i) The Ouse runneth over, as Hamsey Church looks on (Andy Thomas)   ii) The Ouse Valley from the air, showing Malling and Landport (Sussex Express) iii) A dramatic moment, as the rescue helicopter hauls up a stranded Hamsey farmer (Sussex Express)

ON THE FLOOD PLAINS: Now the real meaning of the term 'flood plains' is felt, as the long reclaimed fields between Lewes and Hamsey, always prone to marshiness, are taken back by the Ouse. The lines of the riverbanks have become barely visible. Farmers strive to herd their animals to safety, but in some places there is no high ground to retreat to. A farmer, surrounded by water, has to be hoisted to safety by the rescue helicopter. Sadly, some cattle do drown, and a few bodies even wash up into the town centre. Wildlife along the banks of the Ouse finds its habitats drastically affected, too. Later, perhaps in the atmosphere of blame-seeking which often follows disaster, there is talk that the severity of the Lewes flood was exacerbated by the untimely opening of sluicegates at Barcombe, but this is strenuously denied by authorities.

Typical scene of flood refuse, near Morris Road (Beth Tandy)

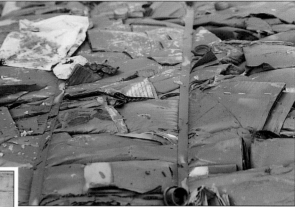

Clockwise from middle: i) Though fairly ineffectual, sandbags become a familiar site throughout Lewes for months ii) Nothing is spared... Mud-soaked kitchenware at Morris Road iii) The force of the water has pushed this wall over at Morris Road iv) Waiting cardboard, now useless, lies damp at the North Street recycling centre (Beth Tandy)

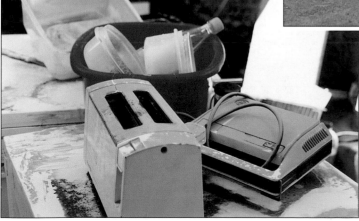

AFTERMATH 1: In the days which follow the disastrous events, the scale of the clean-up operation becomes clear, but feelings of personal loss and a sense of violation take longer to focus. There is a numbness to many affected residents and business owners. Some grit their teeth resolutely and put on brave faces; others are choked, in shock, barely able to voice their inner thoughts. But sooner or later, everyone moves into the inevitable pattern of clearance and renewal.

Now the mundane but necessary task of sorting through personal affects, furniture and utensils is grimly faced. Slowly, recovery begins.

Kiddie's games and videos heartbreakingly nestle with other now-tainted personal belongings (Beth Tandy)

Clockwise from middle: i) Message from a bottle... Muddy detritus becomes a common sight throughout the town (Beth Tandy)   ii) No appointments today... Abandoned hairdresser's chairs in Cliffe (Beth Tandy)   iii) Fashions in a Cliffe precinct shop window which no-one will be buying now   iv) Storehouses at Harveys Brewery take days to drain or pump out (Stephen Crowhurst/Michael Priest)   v) Furniture at Morris Road, once comforting, now ragged remains (Beth Tandy)

AFTERMATH 2: Large piles of ruined belongings start to appear in the streets, the sum of whole lives stacked up unceremoniously for all to see. There is an uncomfortable voyeuristic quality to walking past them. It is the little things which are most affecting, children's once treasured videos and toys, jewellery boxes, ornaments... all are tainted with filthy water and must be destroyed.

Businesses have their own problems; storage areas to be pumped, goods to be replaced, shops to be redecorated after torturous planning applications... Even plaster, soaked with contamination, has to be painstakingly chipped off the walls before trade can recommence. Inevitably, smaller businesses suffer the most.

Cliffe precinct sets about restoration (Beth Tandy)

Clockwise from middle: i) Radio reporter in Morris Road. Media interest in Lewes persists for some time (Beth Tandy) ii) The great clean-up begins (Beth Tandy) iii) A visit from Prince Edward, seen here with Lewes MP Norman Baker to his left (Stephen Crowhurst/Michael Priest) iv) Sweeping polluted mud away... (Beth Tandy)

RECUPERATION: Within a week, Lewes becomes a bustling hive of activity, though the outside world remains inexplicably convinced all is ruined for months and visitors stay away. But this is a time for Lewesians themselves, a space for regeneration and a chance to remind themselves how much this special town means to them as they put it back together, spruced, renewed. Assorted dignitaries and politicians come to visit, Prince Edward, Mo Mowlam *et al.* Media coverage remains high for a while, before the Lewes flood begins to slip into past memory, a realm of local legend seen through the eyes of an odd nostalgia, though fear of a further inundation lurks on. But Lewes will survive, as it has in struggles of ages past - through hell and high water...

The Lewes Flood Appeal

The Lewes Flood Appeal Trust has now helped 273 households with awards totalling £241,780 (over 350 first and second phase awards). The initial phase of awards ensured that households could replace basic goods and necessities damaged in the floods. Careful consideration was given to each application and awards made according to individual circumstances. The second phase took account of the additional costs and losses that everyone incurred to a greater or lesser extent as a result of the floods. We soon realised that the overall losses were greater than the Appeal Fund was able to support, but hoped that the awards made would in some way contribute towards the additional costs and losses. Indeed, as many applicants have said, some losses such as personal items and mementoes can never adequately be replaced. Again, each application was considered individually by the Trustees. The third phase of the Trustees' work will be to use the remaining funds for people who moved away following the floods and are only now returning to hear that an Appeal Fund is available to help them.

On behalf of all the Trustees, I should like to pay tribute to the work of John Magness, the Fund Manager, and his excellent team from Lewes District Council, who have handled the very detailed administration of the Trust with great skill and understanding, and the assessors who volunteered to visit the households affected by the floods. Without the dedication and professional care of all these people the task of the Trustees would have been impossible.

DAVID WADDINGTON
Chairman, Lewes Flood Appeal Trust (Registered Charity No. 1083117)

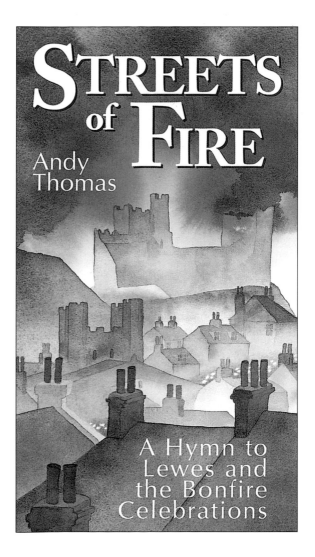

STREETS OF FIRE

A Hymn to Lewes and the Bonfire Celebrations

by Andy Thomas

"Extraordinarily well-written... ...an insight from an insider" **Sussex Express**
"Andy's words will hold strongly in your memory, as will the vivid colour pictures that dot every page of this excellent book" **The Magnet**

Each November the Fifth, the beautiful town of Lewes explodes into a vast pageant of fire which invades the streets as past ages of religious and political upheaval and the general fight for freedom are commemorated. But the rituals also embody more ancient customs in a powerful landscape...

In a personal and impressionistic view, *Streets of Fire* documents the celebrations of one Fifth through the eyes of a Lewesian spectator, roaming the streets to experience the true essence of its mysteriously enchanting drama, moods and humour. With asides and observations, the account reaches to find just why the fires of tradition burn so bright in Lewes, revealing hitherto under-explored aspects of a once sacred landscape which has shaped the lives and customs of its local inhabitants over the centuries.

Illustrated with full colour photographs, and with a foreword by Cliffe Bonfire chairman Andy Freeman, *Streets of Fire* is an evocative and valuable testament to the spirit of a unique town. £5.95, 76pp, S B Publications, ISBN 1-85770-193-3.

This book and many other varied and fascinating regional titles from S B Publications can be easily obtained from all local bookshops. For a full list of S B Publications titles or for direct mail orders, contact:

**S B Publications, 19 Grove Road, Seaford, East Sussex, BN25 1TP.
Tel: 01323 893498/Fax: 01323 893860
e-mail: sales@sbpublications.swinternet.co.uk
Website: www.sbpublications.swinternet.co.uk**

AUTHOR & PHOTOGRAPHERS

ANDY THOMAS: Some Lewes folk will know Andy as the author of *Streets of Fire* (see previous page) which explores the local Bonfire celebrations, but he is familiar to many others as a leading paranormal researcher and author of the books *Fields Of Mystery, Quest For Contact* (with Paul Bura) and *Vital Signs,* acclaimed by many as the definitive guide to the crop circle phenomenon. Andy has also written for magazines and has contributed to and edited a number of books by other writers. He is a founder member of the Southern Circular Research organisation and produced their long-running crop circle journal *SC* for nine years before converting it to the new web site www.swirlednews.com. Andy is a prolific lecturer and speaks widely across England. More recently, he has spoken in Europe and America. He has made numerous radio and TV appearances, including Channel 4's *For The Love Of...,* Meridian ITV's *The Magic & Mystery Show,* BBC 2's *Esther* and ITV's *GMTV* breakfast show.

Andy was born and bred in Lewes, an area he still lives in today with his wife and son. Locally, he is a gigging musician (keyboards) and has also been involved with the popular St Mary's Pantomime in sound and lighting for 19 years.

BETH TANDY: Born in 1982, Beth showed an early interest in photography through family snaps. Suffering from M.E. at seven years old, she was subsequently educated at home. Beth is now studying A-Level photography at Lewes Tertiary College, as well as for qualifications in Art and Design. She is an active volunteer at the Christian Outreach Centre in Brighton and is now official church photographer.

Beth says: "I have lived in Lewes all my life and felt, as a photographer, it was important to record the flood. Without these records, these images would be lost to future generations as would the memories of the people who lived through this sad and tragic incident."

STEPHEN CROWHURST & MICHAEL PRIEST: Steve Crowhurst has lived in Lewes for 40 years and has worked at Harveys for 15 years. Michael Priest has lived in Lewes for 24 years and has worked at Harveys for 23 years. They both work in the same department (bottle stores) and found themselves at the centre of flood events.

Steve says: "Only months before, we had both purchased digital cameras and had taken most of the pictures for the Harveys web site. On the morning of the flood we were both working at the front of the brewery when the river started to come into the yard via the drains. As the water rose, the work force were busy moving equipment to what they thought would be safer levels and we were assigned to moving furniture upstairs. When we returned to our department, the river had started to come inside..." Hence, their valuable photos.

LIZ KAYE ARPS: Liz Kaye moved to her current home in Cliffe High Street, Lewes in 1993. This, of course, placed her right in the middle of the October flood. A music graduate of Sussex University, Liz works in music administration and is a keen singer. She has performed with Sussex and London choirs and has been lucky enough to tour many countries in this capacity. It was through recording her travels on film that her interest in photography began and in 1997 she enrolled on a GCSE photographic course. Two years later she achieved A-Level, grade A, at Lewes Tertiary College. Liz commutes to London, but locally has connections with Cliffe Bonfire Society, St Mary's Pantomime and the Pells Pool.

JENNY KEEN: Jenny Keen has lived in Lewes for 21 years and works in local Further Education. An active member of the Pells Amenity Group, Jenny says: "I was on my way to a meeting with its chairman when I walked along by the Pells lake towards Willeys Bridge. Suddenly, the rising water made the route impassable, and within minutes the Pells Pool and playground were flooded. As the water rose, it entered nearby properties; soon, the whole area had become one vast lake..."